Curriculum Visions

Move on with
Mental maths

Bri... ...n Bass

Curriculum Visions

There's much more online including videos

You will find multimedia resources covering a wide range of topics at:

www.CurriculumVisions.com

CurriculumVisions is a subscription web site.

Series Concept
Brian Knapp, BSc, PhD

Text contributed by
Brian Knapp, BSc, PhD, and Colin Bass, BSc, MA

Editors
Lorna Gilbert, Barbara Carragher, and Gillian Gatehouse

Senior Designer
Adele Humphries, BA, PGCE

Illustrations
David Woodroffe

Designed and produced by
Atlantic Europe Publishing

Printed in China by
WKT Company Ltd

Curriculum Visions Move on with Maths – Mental Maths
A CIP record for this book is available from the British Library

ISBN: 978 1 86214 561 0

Picture credits
All photographs are from the Earthscape Picture Library and ShutterStock collections.

This product is manufactured from sustainable managed forests. For every tree cut down at least one more is planted.

Look out for these sections to help you learn more about each topic:

>>> **Remember...** This provides a summary of the key concept(s) on each two-page entry. Use it to revise what you have learned.

Can you do this? These problems reinforce the concepts learned on a particular spread, and can be used to test existing knowledge.

Answers to the problems set in the 'Move on with Maths' series can be found at: **www.curriculumvisions.com/moveOnAnswers**

Place value

To make it easy for you to see exactly what we are doing, you will find coloured columns behind the numbers in all the examples on this and the following pages. This is what the colours mean:

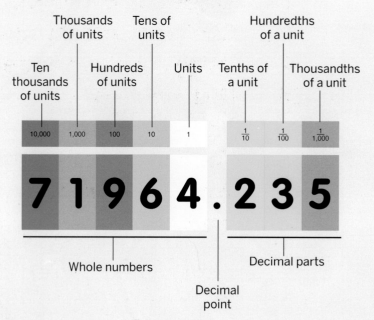

Ten thousands of units	Thousands of units	Hundreds of units	Tens of units	Units	Tenths of a unit	Hundredths of a unit	Thousandths of a unit
10,000	1,000	100	10	1	$\frac{1}{10}$	$\frac{1}{100}$	$\frac{1}{1,000}$

$$7\ 1\ 9\ 6\ 4\ .\ 2\ 3\ 5$$

Whole numbers — Decimal point — Decimal parts

Contents

Using pictures

It often helps to turn numbers into pictures.
Here are some numbers and pictures side by side.

To add **8 + 5**, imagine **8** as a row of **8** counters
and **5** as a row of **5** counters below it:

8 ⬤ ⬤ ⬤ ⬤ ⬤ ⬤ ⬤ ⬤

5   ⬤ ⬤ ⬤ ⬤ ⬤

It is quicker to add in your head easy numbers
like **10**, so imagine taking **2** from the lower row
and adding it to the top row to make a **10**. This
leaves **3** on the bottom row.

10 ⬤ ⬤ ⬤ ⬤ ⬤ ⬤ ⬤ ⬤ ⬤ ⬤

3   ⬤ ⬤ ⬤

In this way we have used pictures in our head
to work out this sum:

$$8 + 5 = 10 + 3 = 13$$

 Remember… The idea is to imagine a number as a
row of pictures. Move the pictures around in your
imagination to get easy numbers like **10** to work with.

Look for short cuts that suit you, as different short cuts suit different people. Here are some more examples. Look at the numbers and also the pictures, if that helps:

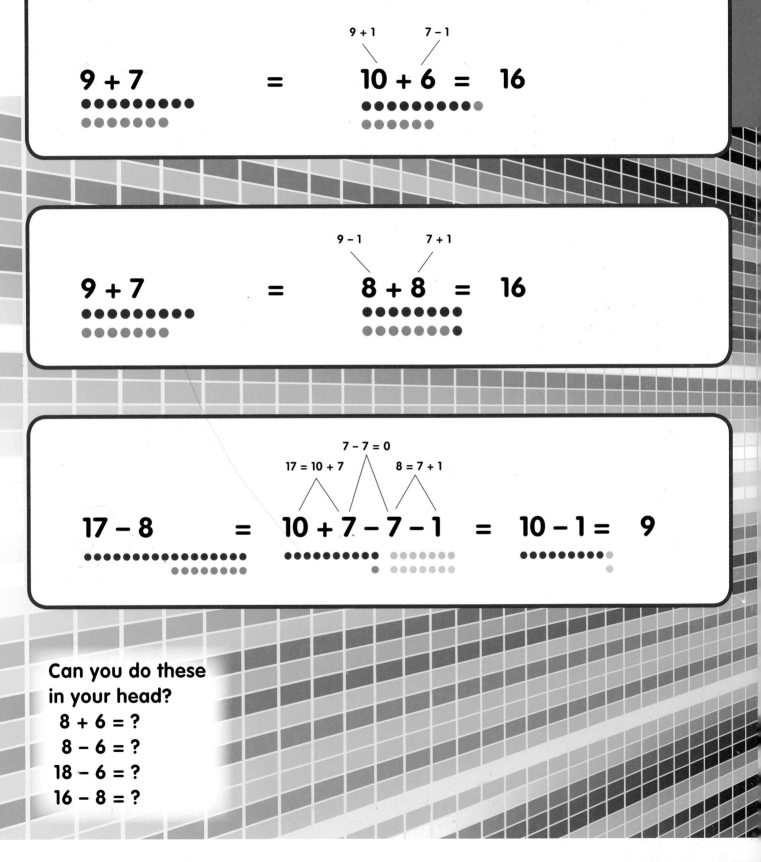

$9 + 7$ = $10 + 6$ = 16

$9 + 1$ $7 - 1$

$9 + 7$ = $8 + 8$ = 16

$9 - 1$ $7 + 1$

$17 - 8$ = $10 + 7 - 7 - 1$ = $10 - 1 = 9$

$17 = 10 + 7$ $7 - 7 = 0$ $8 = 7 + 1$

Can you do these in your head?
$8 + 6 = ?$
$8 - 6 = ?$
$18 - 6 = ?$
$16 - 8 = ?$

Splitting numbers up

The key idea in mental maths is to split up difficult numbers into easy ones.

A large number can be difficult to imagine. But a smaller number is much easier. So, when you see a big number, break it down into smaller ones like this:

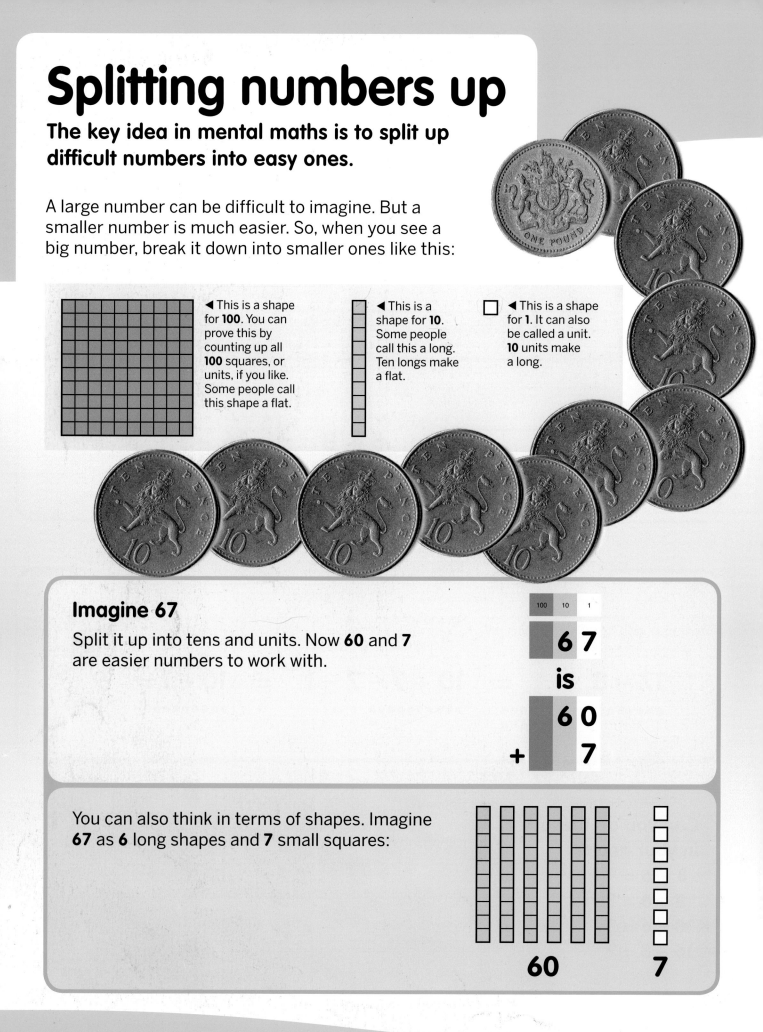

◄ This is a shape for **100**. You can prove this by counting up all **100** squares, or units, if you like. Some people call this shape a flat.

◄ This is a shape for **10**. Some people call this a long. Ten longs make a flat.

◄ This is a shape for **1**. It can also be called a unit. **10** units make a long.

Imagine 67

Split it up into tens and units. Now **60** and **7** are easier numbers to work with.

100	10	1
	6	**7**

is

	6	**0**
+		**7**

You can also think in terms of shapes. Imagine **67** as **6** long shapes and **7** small squares:

60   **7**

Imagine 576
Split up the hundreds, tens and units.

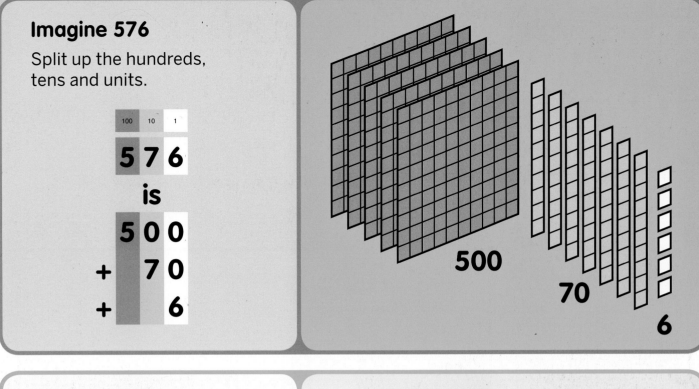

100	10	1
5	7	6

is

	5	0	0
+		7	0
+			6

500

70

6

Imagine 273
Split up the hundreds, tens and units.

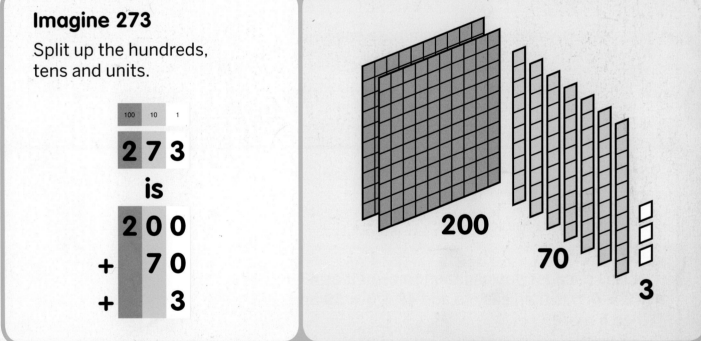

100	10	1
2	7	3

is

	2	0	0
+		7	0
+			3

200

70

3

>>> **Remember...** The key idea in mental maths is to split up difficult numbers into easy ones.

Can you do these? On a separate piece of paper, draw as flats, longs and units:

347

743

473

7

Put the big numbers first

It is often easier to put the bigger number first wherever this is possible. You can do this because of the Turn-Around Rule.

When you are <u>adding</u> two numbers, it is often easier to add the smaller to the larger. For example, working out:

7 + 23 = ?

is easier if you think of it as:

23 + 7

This is partly because you can more easily think of it as **20 + 3 + 7**.

(Answer: **7 + 23 = 23 + 7 = 30**)

▼ If you can think in pictures, this is how you can see the addition.

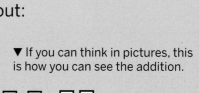

Similarly,

9 + 47 = ?

is easier if you think of it as:

47 + 9

This is because you can then think of it as **47 + 3 + 6**. It is then easy to add **47 + 3 = 50** and then **6** more.

(Answer: **9 + 47 = 47 + 9 = 47 + 3 + 6 = 56**)

▼ If you think in numbers, then imagine the coloured columns.

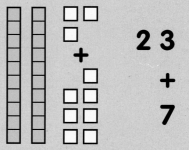

4 and the carried 1 = 5

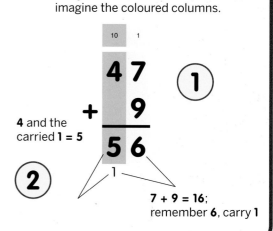

7 + 9 = 16; remember **6**, carry **1**

It also helps to put the big numbers first when you multiply numbers. For example, working out:

4 × 25

is easier if you think of it as:

25 × 4

(Answer: 4 × 25 = 25 × 4 = 100)

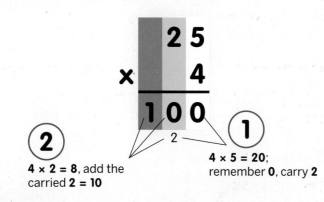

② 4 × 2 = **8**, add the carried **2** = **10**

① 4 × 5 = **20**; remember **0**, carry **2**

Here is another example:

7 × 39

is easier if you think of it as:

39 × 7

(Answer: 30 × 7 + 9 × 7 = 210 + 63 = 273)

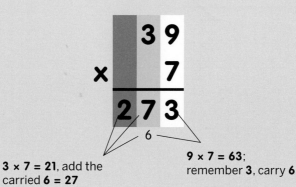

3 × 7 = **21**, add the carried **6** = **27**

9 × 7 = **63**; remember **3**, carry **6**

Can you do these in your head?

6 + 8 = ?

6 + 54 = ?

9 + 33 = ?

8 + 96 = ?

▸▸▸ **Remember...** When adding or multiplying, put the big numbers first to make a calculation easier to work out.

Choosing easy pairs

The more numbers there are to deal with, the harder the problem can seem. We need to organise the problem into easy stages.

One way to do this is to look along the row of numbers and see if we can find easy pairs to do first. Remember, this scheme works only with adding and multiplying.

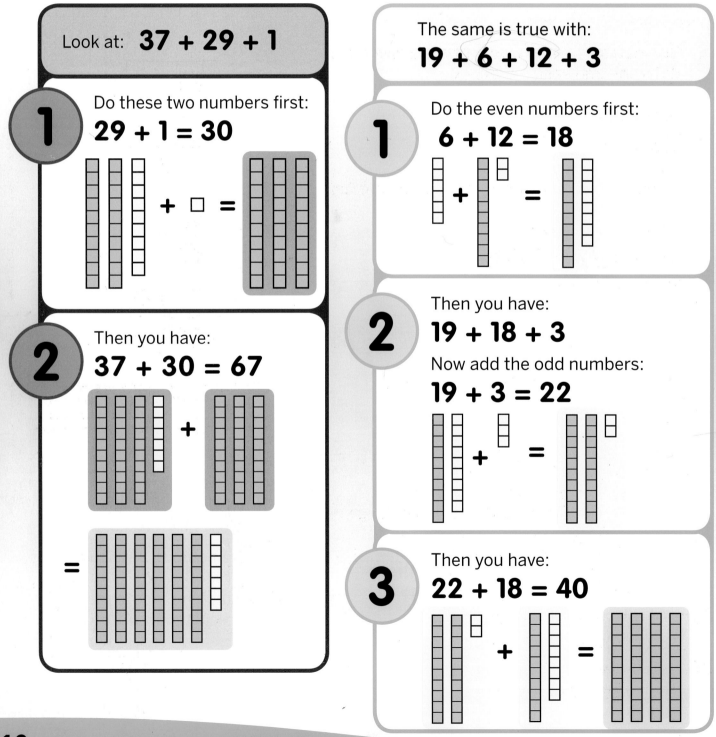

Look at: **37 + 29 + 1**

1 Do these two numbers first:
29 + 1 = 30

2 Then you have:
37 + 30 = 67

The same is true with:
19 + 6 + 12 + 3

1 Do the even numbers first:
6 + 12 = 18

2 Then you have:
19 + 18 + 3
Now add the odd numbers:
19 + 3 = 22

3 Then you have:
22 + 18 = 40

The same principle works with multiplying:

14 × 25 × 4

We could first work out:

14 × 25
(which comes to **350**) and then multiply:

350 × 4
(which comes to **1,400**).

But instead, we can work out the answer in a different, and easier, order.

For example, we know that:

25 × 4 = 100

So we can do this part of the working out first.

Then we can work out:

14 × 100 = 1,400
which is very easy indeed.

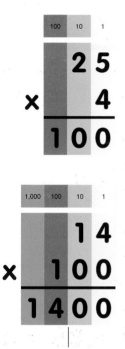

Notice that this multiplication has the bigger number underneath. This is the only time we do this, because multiplying by **100** is simply a matter of adding two **0's** to the first number.

>>> **Remember...** You can add or multiply in any order to make things as easy as possible for yourself.

Can you do these in your head?

19 + 24 + 11 = ?

36 + 13 + 64 + 15 = ?

2 × 12 × 25 = ?

Work with even numbers first

Many problems can be made simpler by working with even numbers first.

For example: **64 + 73 + 36 = ?**

This is a mixture of even and odd numbers.

1 Because it is often easier to work with even numbers first, we group the even numbers together:

64 + 36 + 73 = ?

2 Now add the two even numbers, **64** and **36**:

64 + 36 = 100

or

But if you found this hard to do in your head, you can think of the numbers split up like this:

60 + 4 + 30 + 6

Adding easy pairs (see page 10),

60 + 30 = 90 and **4 + 6 = 10**

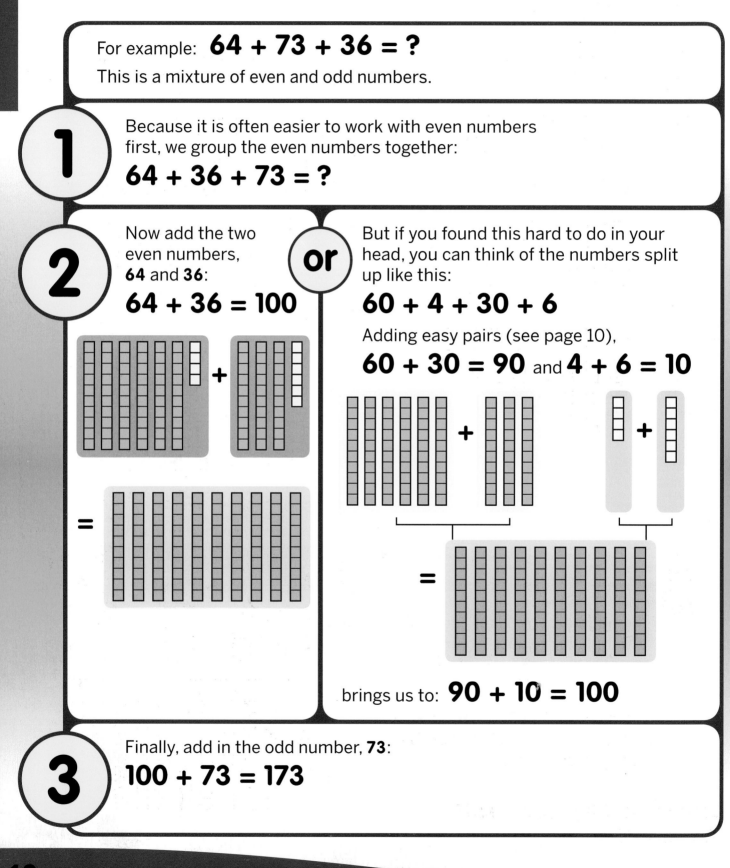

brings us to: **90 + 10 = 100**

3 Finally, add in the odd number, **73**:

100 + 73 = 173

Here is another example: **16 + 29 + 58 = ?**

1

As in the previous example, we rearrange the order in our heads and begin to work out:

16 + 58 + 29 = ?

2

It is easier to add smaller numbers to larger ones, so rearrange again:

58 + 16 = 74

or

Again, if you found this hard to do in your head, you can think of the numbers split up like this:

50 + 8 + 10 + 6

Adding easy pairs:

50 + 10 = 60 and **8 + 6 = 14**

brings us to: **60 + 14 = 74**

3

Now add in the odd number, **29**:

74 + 29
= 70 + 4 + 20 + 9
= 90 + 13 = 103

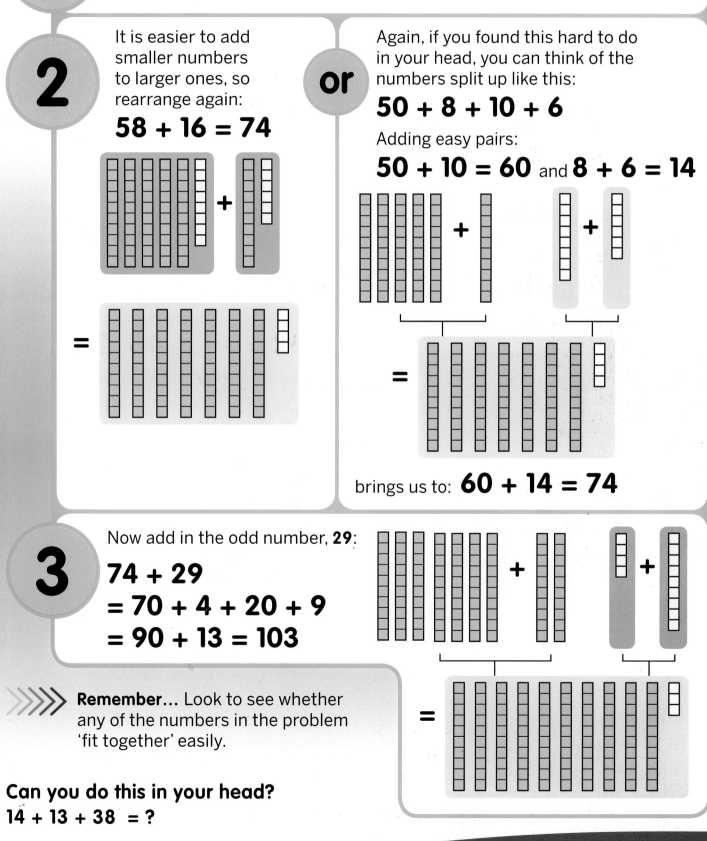

⟫⟫⟫ **Remember...** Look to see whether any of the numbers in the problem 'fit together' easily.

Can you do this in your head?
14 + 13 + 38 = ?

Multiply odd by even numbers

Multiplying can often seem hard because the numbers appear awkward.

Multiplying odd by even helps in simple multiplications like this:

$5 \times 4 \times 3 \times 2 = ?$

Because:

1 $5 \times 4 = 20$

2 and
$3 \times 2 = 6$

3 so
$5 \times 4 \times 3 \times 2$

4 $= 20 \times 6$

5 $= 120$

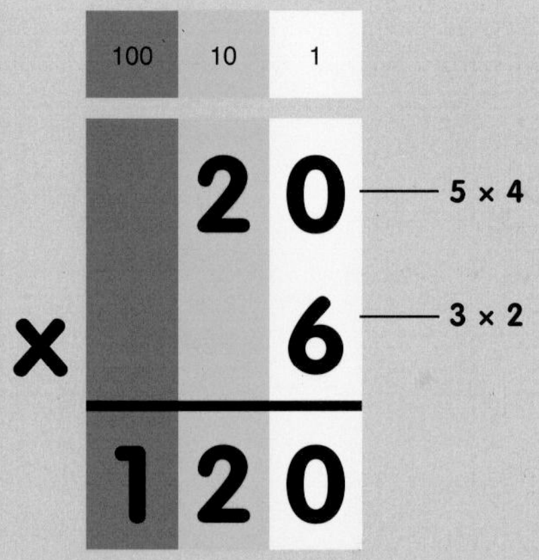

100	10	1	
	2	**0**	— 5×4
×		**6**	— 3×2
1	**2**	**0**	

Can you do these in your head?

$10 \times 9 \times 6 \times 5 = ?$

$3 \times 7 \times 8 \times 6 = ?$

To see why this is easier, let's try multiplying:

$$8 \times 7 \times 6 \times 5 = ?$$

1 $8 \times 7 = 56$

2 $6 \times 5 = 30$

3 We are left with:
56×30

4 As this is a one-line multiplication (**56 × 3**, then add **0** to the answer), it is easy to do in your head.
$= 1,680$

1,000	100	10	1
		5	6	— 7 × 8
×		3	0	— 5 × 6
1	6	8	0
	1		

Suppose for the same sum: $8 \times 7 \times 6 \times 5 = ?$

we had multiplied odds together and evens together?

1 In this case we first multiply the even numbers **8 × 6**:
$8 \times 6 = 48$

2 Then multiply the odd numbers **7 × 5**:
$7 \times 5 = 35$

3 We now multiply the results:
48×35

4 This is much harder to do in your head, as the multiplication on the right shows.
$= 1,680$

| | 4 | 8 | — 6 × 8
| × | 3 | 5 | — 5 × 7
1	4	4	0
	2	4	0
1	6	8	0

>>>> **Remember...** It is worth learning the multiplication facts both ways round. But if you are not sure, you can reverse the numbers to check. For example **8 × 7 = 7 × 8 = 56**.

Quick wits at the market

This story example shows how you can use a number of the ideas we have shown you on the previous pages. Notice that Frances was in a busy market, the sort of place where it is very handy to be able to calculate in your head.

The tea set

Frances had a very pretty porcelain tea set for six people. Over the years three of the cups and three of the saucers had been broken.

One day, while Frances was looking around an antiques market in Cheltenham, she saw a stall selling matching pieces to her tea set quite cheaply. Cups were priced at **£5.60** and saucers at **£3.40**.

Frances told the assistant that she wanted three cups and three saucers. While the assistant was busy with her calculator, Frances checked the answer in her head.

First, she converted the pounds and pence into pence by multiplying by **100**. Then she ignored the currency sign:

5.60 = 560
3.40 = 340

Then, instead of multiplying first, she added first.

She grouped the prices of one cup and one saucer:

560 (a cup) + 340 (a saucer)

Then to calculate the sum, she turned the big numbers into easier ones by splitting up the big numbers:

= 500 + 300 + 60 + 40

Then she added easy pairs:

800 + 100 = 900

Next, because she wanted three cups and three saucers, she multiplied the price of a single cup and saucer by **3**:

900 × 3 = 2,700

Finally, she divided by **100** and put back the currency sign. Frances now knew that she owed **£27.00**.

Can you do this? A loaf costs **£1.49** and a bottle of milk costs **51 pence**. Can you see a quick way to work out in your head the cost of two bottles plus three loaves?

>>> **Remember…** To group numbers, add in the easiest order and then multiply. Always work without decimal points or currency signs.

When adding is better than multiplying

It can be easier to add in what at first seems to be a multiplication problem.

Here we split our numbers to make the multiplication easier, then add the results. You can think of the numbers we use to make the calculation easier as 'stepping stones', making a difficult large single step easier by separating it into a number of smaller steps.

Multiply:

26 × 4 = ?

1

First:

split 26 into 25 + 1

because **25's** are easy to work with.

2

Now we can multiply each part by **4** like this:

25 × 4 = 100
1 × 4 = 4

3

And add the results:

100 + 4 = 104

What is:

$125 \times 5 = ?$

We are going to split the **5** up into **4 + 1** and then split the **125** up into **100 + 25** so that we can use the **4** and the **100** as stepping stones to making our calculation easier.
   Follow these steps:

1 Split the numbers up into:

$$= (125 \times 4) + (125 \times 1)$$
$$= (125 \times 4) + 125$$

2 Now split the **125** into **100** and **25**:

$$= (100 \times 4 + 25 \times 4) + 125$$

125

3 Now work out what is in the brackets:

100 × 4   25 × 4

$$= (400 + 100) + 125$$
$$= 500 + 125$$
$$= 625$$

>>> **Remember...** If the numbers in a problem appear difficult, you might be able to split up one or more of them so that they will be easier to work with.

Can you do these in your head?

$52 \times 6 = ?$
$27 \times 4 = ?$
$128 \times 5 = ?$

Many ways to add

If you split a number up when adding, it often makes a sum easier to work out. There are several ways you can do it.

Here are four ways to work out:

48 + 16 = ?

See which one you find easiest.

Example 1

Think of the:

 **16** as **2 + 14**

So the starting calculation can be shown as:

48 + 2 + 14

Now add easy pairs, **48** and **2**, making the calculation:

50 + 14

Now you have two more simple numbers to add together:

50 + 14 = 64

Example 2

Think of the

 **16** as **20 − 4**

So the starting calculation can be shown as:

48 + 20 − 4

Now add **20** to **48**, making the calculation:

68 − 4

Now you have an easy subtraction:

68 − 4 = 64

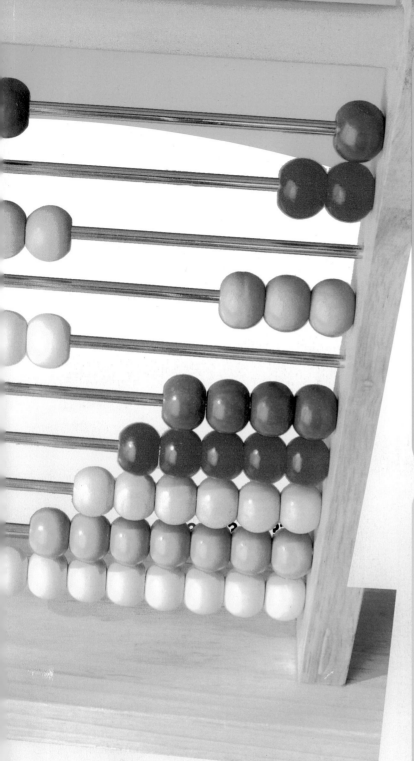

Example 3

Think of the

48 as **50 − 2**

So the starting calculation can be shown as:

50 + 16 − 2

Now add **16** to **50**, making the calculation:

66 − 2

This leaves an easy subtraction:

66 − 2 = 64

Example 4

Think of the numbers as shapes. Imagine adding **2** of the **16** to the **48**, making **50** and leaving **14**.

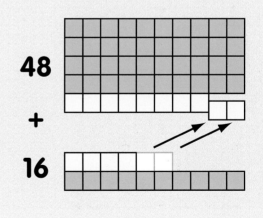

Can you do these in your head?
(try several methods)
24 + 77 = ?
37 + 47 = ?

 Remember... Start by finding an easy way to think about the numbers you are working with.

21

Several ways to subtract

There are several different ways of subtracting in your head. Here the starting numbers have been split differently in each method.

Three ways can be used to work out:

42 − 17 = ?

Example 1

Separate

17 into 12 and 5

So the starting calculation can be shown as:

= 42 − 12 − 5

Now subtract **12** from **42**, which is simple because the last digits are both **2**:

42 − 12 = 30

Finally subtract **5** from the **30**:

= 30 − 5
= 25

 Remember... See if you can separate the starting numbers into numbers that are easier to work with.

Example 2

Separate

17 into 2 and 15

So the starting calculation can be shown as:

42 − 2 − 15

Now subtract **2** from **42**, which is simple because the last digits are the same:

42 − 2 = 40

This makes the calculation:

= 40 − 15
= 25

Example 3

Separate

$\boxed{42}$ into **22** and **20**

So the starting calculation can be shown as:

20 + 22 – 17

Now subtract **17** from **22**, which is **5**:

22 – 17 = 5

This makes the calculation:

= 20 + 5
= 25

**Can you do these
in your head?
(try several methods)
72 – 24 = ?
83 – 25 = ?**

23

Subtracting by adding on

You can find the difference between two numbers by adding on from the smaller one.

We often add on to help check that we are right. For example, if you are given **100** sweets for a party and need only **73**, you might say: **73** and **2** is **75**, and **5** is **80**, and **10** is **90**, and **10** more is **100**. As **2** and **5** and **10** and **10** make **27**, so you know that the difference between **100** and **73** is **27**.

   You can use this adding method to help you do any kind of mental subtraction, for example, to subtract **73 cm** from **100 cm**.

Note: It works best if you are taking away from an easy number, like **100**, or even a much bigger easy number.

Example 1

Katie and Lucy were playing a word game. Katie had **92** points and Lucy had only **37**. How many did Lucy have to score to catch up?

1

Here we are adding on from the smaller number again. Start at **37**. Find a number, such as **3**, that adds to **37** to give an easy number to remember.

37 and 3 is 40

Remember **3** as the first part of our final answer.

2

The next jump can be to add an easy number **50**, which brings us close to **92**.

40 and 50 is 90

Remember **50 + 3 = 53** as the second part of our final answer.

3

Now we only have **2** to go:

90 and 2 is 92

Remember **53 + 2 = 55** as the final part of our answer.

4

So the final answer is:

55 points

Example 2

Mr Filton was waiting for a train home. His watch showed **4:23 pm** and his train was due to leave at **5:04 pm**. How long did he have to wait?

Note: When working out problems which use time we always have to remember that each hour is **60** minutes.

1
Start by adding a small number to get an answer which is an easy number.

23 + 2 = 25   (4:25pm)

Remember **2** as the first part of our final answer.

2
Now add **5** to bring us to the half hour:

25 + 5 = 30   (4:30pm)

Remember **2 + 5 = 7** as the second part of our final answer.

3
Now add on another **30** to bring us to the full hour:

30 + 30 = 60   (5:00pm)

Remember **7 + 30 = 37** as the third part of our final answer.

4
Now we simply have a final **4** to add to bring us to the time the train will leave:

60 + 4 = 64   (5:00pm + 4 = 5:04pm)

Remember **37 + 4 = 41** as the final part of our answer.

5
So the time he has to wait is:

41 minutes

»»» Remember... It is often easier to 'see' the answer to a subtraction by adding upwards from the smaller number. This can also be a good check for subtractions you have written down.

Can you do this in your head? It is **4:44pm** and my next bus home is at **5:13pm**. How long do I have to wait?

25

Subtracting across 100

Here is an easy way to subtract from numbers larger than 100.

Again, it is a matter of making the numbers easy to work out in your head.

To see the difference, compare the way used for doing the calculation in your head to the way it would be done on paper.

What is **133 − 85 = ?**

1 To make the numbers easier to work with, split **133** into **100** and **33**:

$$100 + 33 - 85$$

2 Now, rearrange the calculation so that we can take **85** from **100**:

$$= 100 - 85 + 33$$

3 Next, do the subtraction:

$$(100 - 85) + 33$$

(perhaps you might say **85 plus 5 = 90**, **plus 10 = 100**, answer **15** – this is the 'adding on' method shown on page 24).

$$= 15 + 33$$

4 This leaves the addition:

$$15 + 33 = 48$$

(try **10 + 5 + 30 + 3** to do this. **10 + 30 = 40** and **5 + 3 = 8**, so the answer is **48**).

▼ This is how you would write the problem on paper using the exchanging method of subtracting.

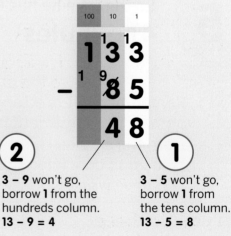

2 3 − 9 won't go, borrow **1** from the hundreds column. **13 − 9 = 4**

1 3 − 5 won't go, borrow **1** from the tens column. **13 − 5 = 8**

Here is another example so that you can see the common steps.

Remember, get the subtraction out of the way by subtracting from an easy number like **100**. Then you are left with an addition, which is easy to do in your head:

159 − 77 = ?

1 To make the numbers easier to work with, split **159** into **100** and **59**:

100 + 59 − 77

2 Now, rearrange the calculation so that we can take **77** from **100**:

100 − 77 + 59

3 Next, do the subtraction:

(100 − 77) + 59

(perhaps you might say **77 plus 3 = 80**, **plus 20 = 100**, answer **23** – this is the 'adding on' method shown on page 24).

= 23 + 59

4 This leaves the addition:

23 + 59 = 82

(try **22 + 1 + 59** to do this **22 + 60**, so the answer is **82**).

▼ This is how you would write the problem on paper using the regrouping method of subtracting.

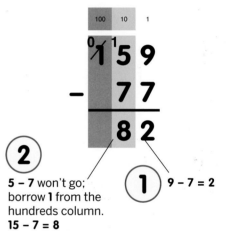

 5 − 7 won't go; borrow **1** from the hundreds column. **15 − 7 = 8**

1 9 − 7 = 2

Can you do these in your head?

132 − 48 = ?

175 − 85 = ?

▶▶▶ **Remember...** To subtract across **100**, first to add to get from the smaller number to **100** and then add the amount the bigger number is above **100**.

Ziggie and Mtoto in Ghana

Ziggie and Mtoto were on holiday in Ghana. On the last afternoon the whole family was looking around the souvenir shops for presents to take back to their friends and relatives. Dad had given each of the twins a 5,000 cedi note to spend.

Both Ziggie and Mtoto found many hand-crafted items they wanted to take home to show their friends. In the end Ziggie found her items cost **3,755 cedi**, and Mtoto found his items cost **2,895 cedi**.

Before they bought them, Ziggie and Mtoto wanted to work out how much change they would get. Here is a way of solving the problem:

(1)

To find Ziggie's change from **5,000 cedi** we are going to add upwards from **3,755**:

$$3,755 + 5 = 3,760$$

Remember **5**.

$$3,760 + 40 = 3,800$$

Now we have added **5 + 40 = 45**, so remember **45**.

$$3,800 + 200 = 4,000$$

Now we have added **200 + 45 = 245**, so remember **245**.

$$4,000 + 1,000 = 5,000$$

In adding upwards to **5,000** we have added **1,000** and **245**, so our answer is **1,245 cedi**.

$$1,000 + 245 = 1,245$$

2

We will also find Mtoto's change from **5,000 cedi** by adding upwards from **2,895**:

$$2,895 + 5 = 2,900$$

Remember **5**.

$$2,900 + 100 = 3,000$$

Now we have added **100 + 5 = 105**, so remember **105**.

$$3,000 + 2,000 = 5,000$$

In adding upwards to **5,000** we have added **2,000** and **105**, so our answer is **2,105 cedi**.

$$2,000 + 105 = 2,105$$

3

To find Ziggie and Mtoto's change, we have to work out:

$$1,245 + 2,105 = ?$$

First, we want to make the numbers easier to work with before we add them in our head.

Add **5** to the first number, and subtract **5** from the second:

$$1,245 + 5 + 2,105 - 5 = ?$$

This gives:

$$1,250 + 2,100 = 3,350$$

So their change was **3,350 cedi**.

Can you do this in your head? What is the change from **£20.00** when you pay:
£9.95
£13.99

Can't remember your tables?

Multiplication tables are single columns of multiplication facts. Put side by side they make a multiplication square.

Most of us forget some parts of our multiplication tables, but here are suggestions of ways to cover up some of the gaps.

Example 1   7 × 8 = ?

1 Start by multiplying using **2's**:
7 × 2 = 14

2 Multiply by **2** again; this is **7 × 4**:
14 × 2 = 28

3 So, by multiplying by **2** three times, you get the same answer as multiplying by **8**.
28 × 2 = 56

Example 2   7 × 9 = ?

1 Multiply by **3**:
7 × 3 = 21

2 Multiply by **3** again:
21 × 3 = 63
(this is **7 × 3 × 3**, or **7 × 9**).
Therefore, by multiplying by **3** twice, you get the same answer as multiplying by **9**.

Here is another way that you can try. If you know that, for example:

7 × 8 = 56

then

7 × 9

is

56 + 7 = 63

Below is a multiplication square to remind you of any gaps you have in numbers up to **9 × 9**. You can copy out and extend this square to **12 × 12** to cover your **12** times tables.

×	1	2	3	4	5	6	7	8	9
1	1	2	3	4	5	6	7	8	9
2	2	4	6	8	10	12	14	16	18
3	3	6	9	12	15	18	21	24	27
4	4	8	12	16	20	24	28	32	36
5	5	10	15	20	25	30	35	40	45
6	6	12	18	24	30	36	42	48	54
7	7	14	21	28	35	42	49	56	63
8	8	16	24	32	40	48	56	64	72
9	9	18	27	36	45	54	63	72	81

Tip... If you cannot remember one multiplication, say **7 × 5**, then think of it the other way around, as **5 × 7**. This is the Turn-Around Rule (see page 8).

>>> **Remember...** The square above can be used to find out basic multiplication facts. Suppose you want to find **3 × 5**, find **3** from the column marked **3** and **5** from the row marked **5**. Now go along the row and column to find where they meet. You will find the answer is **15**.

Can you do these in your head?
3 × 12 = ?
9 × 11 = ?

Using doubles and trebles

Many sports and games need rapid, accurate use of mathematics. In international darts, for instance, you need to be quick at multiplying.

In a singles darts game there are two players, each of whom has three darts, like the ones shown here. The target is a dartboard which is hung on a wall. It is marked off in numbered sectors, as you can see.

The players take turns to stand a fixed distance from the board and throw their darts into it.

Usually, each player starts with a score of **501**. The score for each three darts is added up and then subtracted from the remaining score. The first player to reach zero wins.

However, there are some special areas on the board where you can get a bigger score. These are the triple (three times) and double (two times) rings.

The winner must finish by throwing a dart into a double (that means if the dart lands in double **19**, the score is **38**).

Double ring

Triple ring

⟫ **Remember...** For speedy answers, split up big numbers into simpler ones.

It was Wayne's turn in the darts game. He had to score **113**. First he had to score an odd number, so that the remainder would be an even number, and he could finish on a double. If he scored triple **11** with his first dart, he planned to finish on two double **20's**. First, triple **11**.

$$11 \times 3 = 33$$
$$113 - 33 = 80$$

And then the **2** double **20's**.

$$(20 \times 2) + (20 \times 2) = 80$$

Unluckily, he just missed triple **11**. Instead the dart went into triple **14**. Now he had to do some more quick mental maths:

His score was now:

$$3 \times 14 = 42$$

$3 \times (10 + 4) = 30 + 12$

$$113 - 42 = 71$$

$110 - 40 + 3 - 2 = 70 + 1$

If he hit triple **11** this time, his score would become:

$$71 - 33 = 38$$

$60 + 11 - 30 - 3$

Now, **38** is double **19**.
Again he missed and instead hit triple **19**, which is an odd number.
Triple **19** is:

$$3 \times 19 = 57$$

$3 \times (20 - 1) = 60 - 3$

Wayne used 'counting back' to find out what he had to score now:

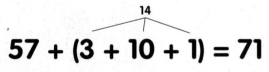

$$57 + (3 + 10 + 1) = 71$$

so he had to score:

14

Now, double **7** would do, and to his delight, this is exactly what he got!

Can you do these in your head?
Using three darts, and finishing on a double, find a way to score:
103
39

Near doubles

Doubling can often save time. Here is how to use doubling when the numbers to multiply are just 1 apart.

Two tourists, Susie and Tom, went to Orlando, Florida, and found they needed new sunglasses. They saw a matching pair they liked. The ladies' style cost **$16**, but the men's version cost **$17**. The two prices were just **1** apart.

Susie worked out the total by doubling the first number and adding **1**.

$$16 \times 2 + 1$$
$$= 32 + 1$$
$$= 33$$

This is the 'near-double' principle.

Or, Susie could have worked out:

$$17 \times 2 - 1$$
$$= 34 - 1$$
$$= 33$$

That is, she could have doubled the second number and then subtracted **1**.

Note: The $ sign before a number means dollars.

```
    1 6
 +  1 7
 ─────
    3 3
    1
```

Near doubles, halving and adding

Susie and Tom were expecting to pay **$33** for their sunglasses, but they knew that sales tax had to be added on. It was **6%**. Tom checked the amount of the tax like this:

$$6\% = (5 + 1)\%$$

Now, **5%** is half of **10%**, and **10%** of **33** is a tenth of **33.00**, or **3.30**:

This meant that Tom could calculate that if **10%** of **33.00** is **3.30**, then **5%** is half of **3.30**:

$$\frac{3.30}{2} = 1.65$$

And because **1%** is a tenth of **10%** then he worked out that **1%** of **33** was:

$$\frac{3.30}{10} = 0.33$$

By adding these two answers together Tom worked out that **6%** tax on **$33** is **$1.98**:

$$1.65 + 0.33 = 1.98$$

The total cost of the sunglasses was therefore the price (**$33**) plus the sales tax (**$1.98**). This was **$34.98**.

Can you do these in your head?
What is the sales tax at **10%** on **$33**?
What is the sales tax at **7.5%** on **$33**?
(Remember that **5%** is half of **10%**, and **2.5%** is half of **5%**.)

Remember... Splitting up numbers to make doubles can save time and make numbers easier to work with.

More near equals

If you can remember square numbers, here you have another way to remember awkward multiplication facts.

Imagine that we have a square like a chess board.

It is **8 × 8 = 64**

Then we cut one row of squares off the edge. Next, we stick that row along another edge. Our square then becomes a rectangle of **9** units (or squares) by **7**, with an odd bit sticking out at the corner.

We cut this odd bit off and throw it away.
   The area of the rectangle we have made is **9 × 7**. This is **64 − 1**, because we took one square away.

So **9 × 7 = 63**

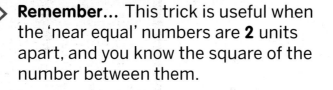

>>>> **Remember...** This trick is useful when the 'near equal' numbers are **2** units apart, and you know the square of the number between them.

You could do this starting with a square of any size. For example:

$$6 \times 6 - 1 = 7 \times 5$$
$$4 \times 4 - 1 = 5 \times 3$$

You can see that by cutting the edge off a square as we did on page 36, that this trick works however big the numbers are. So now we know that:

$$19 \times 21 = 20 \times 20 - 1$$
$$= 400 - 1$$
$$= 399$$

and:

$$16 \times 14 = 15 \times 15 - 1$$
$$= 225 - 1$$
$$= 224$$

and:

$$99 \times 101 = 100 \times 100 - 1$$
$$= 10,000 - 1$$
$$= 9,999$$

When you come across a large square number, it is worth trying to remember it for use in this trick.

Can you work out the connection between these in your head? 6 x 8 and 7 x 7?

Look at the multiplication square on page 31 to see other connections like this.

The Wordsmith's card game

Here is an example where you can use many of the mental maths rules you have seen on the previous pages. They are set out below as part of a family card game.

The Wordsmith family is playing a card game. Each player has seven letter cards and takes turns to make up a sort of a crossword.

It is Ziggie's turn, and she thinks she can make an eight-letter word using an **L** already on the board and adding an **A** to **WASH** to make it **AWASH**. If she can do this, she can score **173** points.

At present, Ziggie's father is in the lead with **335** points, and Ziggie is second with **166**.

Will Ziggie overtake her father?

To find out, we need to know if:

335 – 166 is bigger than 173

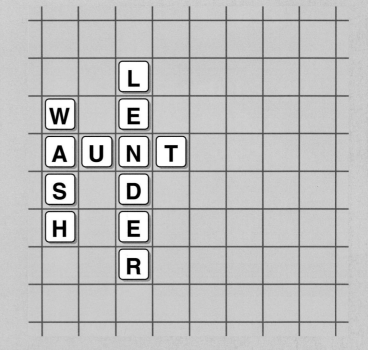

First find some 'stepping stones' to make the subtraction easier. In this case we will use **300** (because it is close to **335**) and **200** (because it is close to **166**) as 'stepping stones' to the answer. Remember, we have to add and subtract the **300** and the **200** to leave the equation unchanged.

$$= 335 + (-300 + 300) + (-200 + 200) - 166$$

Now we can take away more easily:

$$= (335 - 300) + (300 - 200) + (200 - 166)$$

(**335 – 300 = 35; 300 – 200 = 100**). To find **200 – 166**, we count up:
4 to **170** and **30** more to **200**.

$$= 35 + 100 + (4 + 30)$$

Now use the Turn-Around Rule to add numbers in the easiest order:

$$= 100 + 35 + 34$$

And finally, because **35** and **34** are close, use the technique of near doubles (**35 + 34 = 35 × 2 – 1**):

$$= 100 + 35 \times 2 - 1$$
$$= 169$$

Since **173** is bigger than **169**, a score of **173** would just put Ziggie into the lead. So she decides to risk it and puts down the cards to spell **ATLANTIC**.

Can you do this in your head? Ziggie's Mum has **151 points**. She has these letters: **P E U R O**. If she can use them all this turn, she will score **29 points** and then her total score will be doubled because they are the last letters. Can she overtake Ziggie?

What symbols mean

Here is a list of the common maths symbols together with an example of how they are used.

+ The symbol for adding. We say it 'plus'. In Latin plus means 'more'.

– Between two numbers this symbol means 'subtract' or 'minus'. In front of one number it means the number is a minus number. In Latin minus means 'less'.

= The symbol for equals. We say it 'equals' or 'makes'. It comes from a Latin word meaning 'level' because weighing scales are level when the amounts on each side are equal.

$$(8 + 9 - 3) \times \frac{2}{5} = 5.6$$

( ) The symbols for brackets. You do everything inside the brackets first. Brackets always occur in pairs.

× The symbol for multiplying. We say it 'multiplied by' or 'times'.

—, / and ÷ Three symbols for dividing. We say it 'divided by'. A pair of numbers above and below a / or — make a fraction, so $^2/_5$ or $\frac{2}{5}$ is the fraction two-fifths.

. This is a decimal point. It is a dot written after the units when a number contains parts of a unit as well as whole numbers. This is the decimal number five point six.

Index